LAVENDER JESSAMINE

MEMORIES OF A HEART ON THE MEND

ANDERSON BANKS JR.

LAVENDER JESSAMINE

Anderson Banks Jr.
Lavender Jessamine

Published by Spines
ISBN: 979-8-89569-778-8

PROLOGUE: THERAPY SESSION

It's Wednesday, two o'clock in the afternoon, and Andrew finds himself once again "On The Couch" for his weekly therapy session. Journaling has played a crucial role in lifting his spirits, rating his current mood at an impressive eight out of ten. He's been consistent with his medication, and recently, a new companion has joined his life: a one-month-old Pitbull Husky Mix gifted to him that he proudly named Kobe.

"I feel like an onion wrapped in layers of emotions, flashbacks, loneliness, and somber thoughts,"

Andrew shared with his therapist.

"That's a powerful analogy,"

She replied.

"Can you elaborate on that?"

Andrew continued,

"Each of these layers reflects the mental and emotional turmoil that brought me to my suicide attempt in high school."

- **Verbal Abuse**
- **Emotional Abuse**
- **Psychological Abuse**
- **Mental Anguish**
- **Slanderous Words From My Mother**
- **First Love**
- **First Heartbreak**
- **Anxiety**
- **Depression**
- **Panic Attacks**
- **Extremely Introverted Personality Traits**

- **Highly Sensitive Nature**

"As I continue to write in my journal, attend our therapy sessions, and take my medication, I find clarity emerging as those layers are gradually peeled away. It's as if the 'curtain' is being pulled back, allowing me to see clearly for the first time in forty years. I realize that while I cannot change the abuse of my childhood, I can strive to understand my mother's misguided intentions. I've always wanted her to see me as a human being, and now I realize that I must also see her as a human being —an 'Imperfect Being' capable of errors and filled with sorrow!"

They continued the session when the therapist asked,

"How did you manage to complete Marine Corps boot camp with all the stress that is involved?"

After a five-second pause, Andrew responded,

"In boot camp, I realized that I have the ability to compartmentalize certain situations."

"I immediately understood that all of the actions, yelling, name-calling, and cursing from my Drill Instructors were never personal."

"My Drill Instructors were not responsible for raising and nurturing me… that was my mother's job."

"My mother's actions were personal, while the 'Drill Instructors' behavior was strictly business."

"What made you join the Marine Corps?"

She asked.

"Well,"

Andrew said calmly,

"The main reason I joined the Marine Corps was to prove my mother wrong. I wanted her to know and understand how tough I really am. Being a hypersensitive introvert does not make someone a weak person, and I had to show her that."

He continued,

"My two brothers-in-law were both Active Duty Marines at the time, and I wanted to emulate them as well. Also, as pathetic as it might have sounded at the time, I was still madly in love with Dianna Marshall, and my broken heart didn't want to live in the same city that she lived in. Finally, I was desperate to leave Mississippi."

"If I couldn't go back home to Miami, the next best choice was to join the military, and the Marine Corps was my first and only choice."

His therapist listened intently while taking notes.
She added,

"Those are some strong motivating factors!"

Andrew's therapist asked one final question.

"How was Marine Corps boot camp?"

Andrew answered,

"I wrote about my entire boot camp experience in my journals!"

Over the next several weeks,
Andrew took his therapist on a journey, yet again, to
the past while he told her about:

**The summer of 1983 and
Marine Corps Boot Camp!**

'83 SUMMER VACATION

Andrew was eagerly anticipating his upcoming summer vacation, where he'll visit his sisters in Oceanside and San Diego, CA.

He was determined to achieve one main goal during his time away:

"Get in the best shape possible to be physically prepared for Marine Corps boot camp."

He's a few months past his suicide attempt and is slowly moving on with his life.

He looked back at that moment and thought,

"WOW; I'M LUCKY TO STILL BE ON
THIS EARTH AFTER WHAT I DID."

Although he was accepting the reality of his first heartbreak, Andrew continued to grapple with lingering feelings for Dianna Marshall. Despite being unable to forget or stop entirely loving his first love, he strived to view it as a valuable learning experience. Andrew was working hard to adopt a new outlook on life.

"Life goes on, and it's time to live it!"
"Time waits for no one!"
**"It's better to have loved and lost than to have
never loved at all!"...**

All The Cliches Used In An Attempt To Mend A Broken Heart! (*It Didn't Work!*)

Andrew arrived in San Diego a few weeks later and breathed in the fresh air.

"IT AIN'T MIAMI,"

He thought,

"BUT IT'S STILL A BEAUTIFUL CITY."
FIRST THINGS FIRST, "WHERE IS THE
NEAREST GYM?"

His brother-in-law Larry was a Drill Instructor at Marine Corps Recruit Depot (MCRD) San Diego. The next day, he took Andrew to the Marine Corps Base and showed him around. Larry introduced him to a few Drill Instructors, and they gave him advice pertaining to getting through boot camp.

"Don't take the yelling and screaming personally!"

"Marines are the best fighters in the world, and one doesn't become a Marine without being tested to the max." When the Drill Instructors told him about Marines being the best of the best, his face beamed with pride. "Wow… I will be among the Best Of The Best!"

Next, Larry took him to the Base Gym. The gym was huge! Various rooms consist of free weights, a variety of machines for weight training, a basketball court, a room with cardiovascular equipment, a sauna, and a whirlpool. Andrew brought his training gear and began training alongside the Marines in the gym.

He discovered his passion for bodybuilding at the age of twelve after being inspired by the TV series The Incredible Hulk. With his quiet disposition, he often saw himself in the character of David Bruce Banner, while the Hulk became his personal Alter Ego, a protector against the abuse he endured throughout his youth. Lou Ferrigno, who portrayed the Hulk, became Andrew's hero, inspiring his desire for formidable muscles like those of the iconic green giant.

Andrew channeled his admiration for Comic Book Superheroes into art, drawing The Incredible Hulk on anything he could find, even decorating his bedroom wall with several renditions of the character.

He drew versions of Spiderman, too... but that ain't important... He's just trying to boast about his hidden drawing talent! LOL!!

His mom saw the drawings and she loved them.

"I didn't know that you could draw like that,"

She told him.

At that moment, he thought,

"I WISH THAT MOM AND I HAD A
STRONG MOTHER/SON
RELATIONSHIP."

Mom bought him his first weight set when he was twelve, and Andrew became a bodybuilding fanatic. Now that he had access to the Base Gym,

"I'm gonna pack on some serious muscle before I head back to Visalia! Every moment that I spend in the gym will be a step closer to transforming myself into my own superhero! I want my body to be powerful and unrecognizable!"

At just eighteen, Andrew found himself training alongside Marines, who were in their mid to late twenties.

The Marines training in the gym were familiar with his brother-in-law Larry and decided to take young Andrew "Under Their Wing," guiding him through intense workouts to prepare for boot camp.

"You're gonna be 'More Than Ready' for boot camp when we finish with you,"

They told him.

Some of the Marines were off-duty Drill Instructors, and they screamed and yelled at Andrew during their training sessions.

"We're gonna acclimate you as to what you will face in boot camp!"

Each weekday, Larry would drop Andrew off at the gym, where he trained ferociously while being disparaged by the Drill Instructors. After completing his training for the day, Andrew took the local city bus back to his sister's house.

Several weeks later, he went to Oceanside, CA, where his brother-in-law Will was stationed at Marine Corps Base Camp Pendleton. Will was a hardcore bodybuilder at the time and had muscles "Coming Out Of His Ears!" Will became Andrew's first hero and role model when he was just nine years old, inspiring Andrew to emulate him in every way possible.

As a testament to his reverence, Andrew even mimicked Will's distinctive bowlegged walk during his younger years.

"Stop trying to walk like Will,"

His brother Perry would say while laughing at him.

Will took Andrew to his local gym, which was filled with amateur and professional bodybuilders. He met professional bodybuilder John Brown, who had won the Mr. Universe title on multiple occasions. He had never been up close to a professional bodybuilder, and "WOW!" ... " Impressive!" John was super nice, and he showed Andrew multiple training exercises and training methods.

Andrew's days consisted of eating, sleeping, and training...wash, rinse, and repeat! Thanks to Mr. Universe, he learned a lot about proper nutrition to gain muscle. His brother-in-law Will and his sister Joyce stocked the freezer with chicken, fish, and steak.

Andrew also had a steady supply of healthy carbohydrates that included white rice, brown rice, white potatoes, sweet potatoes, and pasta. Will took him to the local vitamin supplement store and bought him the same protein powders and supplements that he was using at the time for bodybuilding competitions. His family made sure that he had the proper food and nutrition to build a muscular frame.

Along with training, Andrew had multiple private talks with his sisters and brothers-in-law. Aware of his naturally reserved nature, they expressed concerns about his decision to join the Marine Corps.

Oblivious to Andrew, his mother didn't want him to join the Marines.

"Mom is very afraid that you're not tough enough to complete Marine Corps boot camp,"

His sisters told him.

"She said that you're too quiet and sensitive and that you won't be able to handle the stress,"

Mom told them about his two panic attacks and the hospital emergency room visits.

Thankfully, she didn't tell them about his suicide attempt.

Tears welled up in his eyes as he addressed his family with a newfound sense of authority.

"I'm going to make it through boot camp!"

"I might be a very quiet and sensitive person, but I have an Inner Strength that Mom knows nothing about!"

By this point in his life, Andrew found himself weary of the constant need to justify his withdrawn nature. It had become a familiar refrain, a tired back-and-forth with family members who often failed to grasp the true depth of his personality.

He no longer saw his quiet demeanor as a flaw but rather as a unique strength that fostered deep reflections.

He longed for his mother to recognize that being reserved was not merely about shying away from the spotlight but about embracing solitude as a pathway to understanding the world and himself.

This realization gave him a sense of empowerment, and he wished for 'Mom' to see that underneath his calm exterior lay a reservoir of strength and insight.

"Quiet Doesn't = Soft, and I'm tired of being looked at as odd or different!"

As his sisters and brothers-in-law observed him, they couldn't help but notice the glistening tears in his eyes, a raw testament to the intensity of his feelings. Each word he uttered carried a weight that resonated not only in his voice but also in the gestures of his body language.

Andrew, on the verge of transformation, was building a physique that grew leaner and more muscular through the relentless demands of his rigorous bodybuilding training. This newfound strength was not merely physical; it surged through him, instilling a confidence that blossomed as he built not only his muscles but a fortified sense of self-worth, evolving into a man who not only felt bigger and stronger but who could also face the world with his head held high.

His family replied,

"Andrew, you have the right attitude, and we have no doubt that you will complete boot camp and become a U.S. Marine!"

Those positive words from his family gave him an extra boost of motivation, and he was ready to take on The Ultimate Challenge!

Andrew returned to Visalia with an extra fifteen pounds of muscle spread over his entire body. He left Visalia for CA weighing 175lbs and returned weighing 190lbs. His strength had "Shot Through The Roof!" His bench press went from 195lbs to 325lbs. His squat was 200lbs and is now 400lbs. His deadlift went from 225lbs to 425lbs.

He chuckled to himself,

"I'M THE INCREDIBLE HULK NOW!"

He had a quick slip into the past when he thought,

"I SHOULD WALK BY DIANNA'S HOUSE SO THAT SHE CAN SEE ALL THIS MUSCLE THAT I'VE GAINED OVER THE SUMMER!"

He immediately shook the thought out of his head and went to visit a few neighborhood friends instead.

"Andrew, what did you do?"

His friends were amazed at his new muscular physique.

"Yeah, I'm ready for Marine Corps boot camp!"

Along with spending time with friends, Andrew reached out to his favorite uncle, who lived in Richmond, VA. His uncle's last name was Burns, and all of his nieces and nephews called him Uncle Burney. Uncle Burney was a retired Army Sergeant Major who had multiple tours of Vietnam during the Vietnam War. Uncle Burney promised Andrew,

"I'll write you while you're in boot camp, and I will also come to Parris Island for your graduation!"

August 22, 1983... The Marine Corps recruiter arrived at Andrew's house. It's time to go to boot camp. The recruiter talked with Andrew's mother for a few minutes. Before leaving home, Andrew looked at his mom in the eyes as he spoke from his heart.

"I Love You Mom,"

Followed by a big hug and a kiss on the cheek.

It was a solemn moment between Mother and Son. Andrew had never told his mom, "I Love You!" Nor had he ever shown her any type of affection. Deep in the back of his mind, Andrew saw it as a "Final Goodbye!" As he slid into the front passenger seat of the recruiter's car, Andrew glanced back at his mom and noticed a tear rolling down her cheek. At that moment, his thoughts drifted to his childhood, longing for a closer bond with her.

After Andrew left, his mother went to the living room to look at the family photo albums. She smiled as she looked at photos of Andrew Sr. playing with his newborn son Andrew Jr. The photos took her on a journey of Andrew's life.

"He's always been a good kid,"

Mom thought to herself.

"I'm so embarrassed for treating him so terribly!"

"He deserved much better!"

Her grave thoughts weighed heavy on her heart as mom continued looking through Andrew's life in pictures.

"I wish that I could raise him all over again,"

Were her final thoughts as she closed the photo album.

The recruiter drove Andrew to the recruiting station in Jackson, MS, to complete some final paperwork. Afterwards, he drove Andrew to the Jackson Municipal Airport.

"THIS IS MY FIRST TIME ON A PLANE,"

He thought, while he boarded the plane along with the other passengers. As the plane taxied down the runway, Andrew was eerily relaxed. He reclined his seat to rest during the flight.

Several hours later, they landed at an airport somewhere in South Carolina.

Andrew exited the plane and was ushered to a small commuter plane with the capacity to fly ten passengers. The small plane landed at an airfield, and Andrew disembarked. He was then escorted to a bus full of young men just like him.

AND OFF THEY WENT!

THE BUS RIDE

ANDREW WALKED DOWN THE AISLE OF THE BUS, observing all the young men who were on the same journey as himself.

"A busload of boys contemplating the task ahead on the road to becoming men!"

They all had long heads full of hair; Andrew included, who wore a medium-sized afro with side-burns down his face.

He took a seat, and the driver began the drive to Marine Corps Recruit Depot (MCRD) Parris Island. The number one topic of conversation among the young men was,

"Where are you from?"

They shouted out a variety of cities throughout the United States.

"I'm from Atlanta!"

"I'm from The Bronx; BX All Day Baby!"

"Detroit In 'Da House!"

"Visalia, MS,"

Says Andrew.

"Oh, we got a Country Boy on the bus,"

Says one of the young recruits.

Ninety minutes later, the bus drove under an arch with a sign that read:

Welcome To MCRD Parris Island!

The military police waved the bus through the gate. Andrew felt tension creeping in, so he took slow, deep breaths to calm himself.

"I CAN DO THIS!"

He said to himself.

The driver pulled the bus in front of a large building and turned off the engine. Outside the bus, a row of yellow footprints marked the sidewalk. Three Marines in camouflage uniforms emerged from the building and descended the steps. Two Marines took their positions outside the bus, while the third Marine boarded.

He paced up and down the aisle, casting a menacing stare at each young man before returning to the front and slowly turning to face the recruits.

"Welcome To Parris Island!"...

"You Idiots Have Ten Seconds To Get Off This Damn Bus, And Eight Of Them Are Gone!"

"MOVE! MOVE! MOVE!"

Andrew and the rest of the recruits scattered off the bus into the sights of the two awaiting Marines.

"GET YOUR STINKING FEET ON THOSE FOOTPRINTS NOW!"

"MOVE DAMNIT!"

"MOVE!"

"MOVE YOUR SLOW ASSES NOW!"

Andrew stood on the first set of yellow footprints available as everyone else lined up.

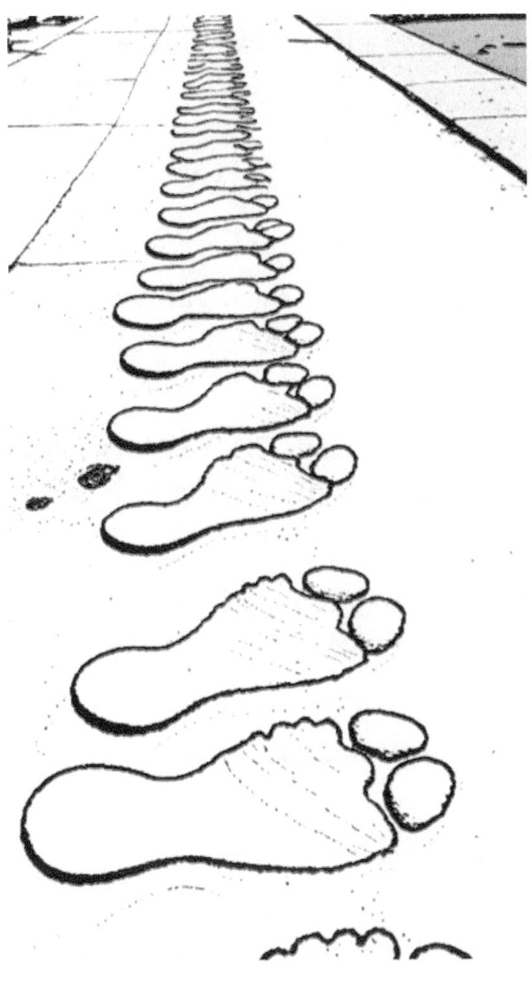

"LOCK 'YO STINKIN' BODIES UP!"

Andrew gave himself a quick reminder,

"THIS IS BUSINESS; NOT
PERSONAL!"

The three Marines stood at the top of the stairs overlooking the new recruits. The Marine in charge stepped forward.

"YOU DON'T BELONG TO 'YA MOMMIES AND 'YA DADDIES ANYMORE GENTLEMEN!"

"YOU ARE NOW PROPERTY OF THE UNITED STATES MARINE CORPS!"

"THAT MEANS YOU BELONG TO ME!"

He continued speaking...

"This is just the beginning of your journey to become a member of the most elite fighting unit in the world!"

"You are now in the Receiving Platoon!"

"You will go through the process that will get you all *ready for Basic Training!*"

He then ordered,

"Now everyone turn to the right."

"In a single file, walk up the stairs and into the room where the other Marines are standing."

"QUICKLY! QUICKLY! QUICKLY!"

UUMMM...BEFORE YOU CONTINUE, I HAVE TO REMIND YOU THAT THIS IS PG 13!

EDIT YOURSELF A LITTLE ON SOME OF THE CUSSIN' FROM THE DRILL INSTRUCTORS!

WE KNOW HOW MUCH CUSSIN' THAT GOES ON IN MARINE CORPS BOOT CAMP!

OK! I WILL!

CARRY ON!

CARRY ON! AYE AYE SIR!

RECEIVING PLATOON

THE RECRUITS SAT ON THE FLOOR AS THE THREE Marines took center stage. The senior Marine stepped forward...

"Welcome To Parris Island Gentlemen!"

"Today Is The First Day Of The Rest Of Your Miserable Lives!"

He paced back and forth, continuing his introductory speech as the Marine recruits listened.

"First, Gentlemen, you will be receiving your initial uniform supply, personal hygiene kits, and a variety of necessities!"

"If you all follow directions, this process will go along very smoothly!"

The group lined up, standing shoulder to shoulder, as ordered. They side-stepped to the right as military uniforms, boots, and various kits were placed in their outstretched arms.

Now, every Marine, Active Duty and Retired, has several funny boot camp stories. Andrew definitely has a few of his own!

"OK, Gentlemen,"

Says the Marine in charge;

"Take off those civilian clothes and put on your camouflage uniform!"

The men began getting undressed to change clothes. A spooky silence enveloped the room when...

"WHAT THE F***IS THAT!!!"

Everyone stopped what they were doing, and looked to see what was going on. The Marine walked up to a single individual. He stared at the young man up and down as the remaining recruits began to see the problem. They fought to hold in their laughter.

"BOY,"

Said the senior Marine;

"WHAT 'DA HELL ARE YOU WEARING?"

Before the recruit could answer, the Marine continued with,

"ARE YOU WEARING WOMEN'S PINK PANTIES?"

"Please tell me that YOU ARE NOT wearing women's pink panties!"

The Marine gave the recruit time to speak.

"Yes Sir, I'm wearing pink panties, Sir!"

"I like how the silk feels on my skin, Sir!"

Guys were laughing into their hands to avoid an outburst.

HAHAHA!!!!

Shaking his head in confusion, the Marine in charge yelled,

"Hurry up and get outta that shit before I take you to get your ears pierced!"

Andrew whispered to the recruit beside him,

"If he's wearing pink panties, chances are that his ears are already pierced!"

Laughter erupted as Andrew's whispering was louder than he thought.

"Line Up," was their next set of instructions. The recruits fell in line wearing boots, camouflage pants, and a white T- shirt. The T- shirts given to Andrew were a size too small. He stood there with his newly built muscles protruding when the senior Marine set his sights on him. Andrew stood at attention while the Marine paced in front of him.

"Aaaaahhhh…We got us a Hercules over here!"

He stood nose-to-nose with Andrew.

"You think all those muscles make you tough, don't you?"

Andrew shouted,

"SIR, NO SIR!"

"Because all those muscles don't mean shit…you're still trash!"

"DO YOU UNDERSTAND ME?"

"SIR, YES SIR,"

Replied Andrew…

"THEN SAY IT!"

As loud as he could, Andrew shouted,

"THE RECRUIT IS TRASH, SIR!"

And now he is hoping for the spotlight to be off of him. It was Andrew's turn to be laughed at by the rest of the room. LOL!!

The recruits took a seat on the floor as the Marine in charge sat on a stool.

He lectured them on the upcoming events. He was speaking as they listened when... a very familiar sound interrupted the lecture.

"BBbbbrrrrrRRRRRTTTTT"

The odor of sulfur and rotten eggs filled the room.

The Marine stood up while kicking the stool to the floor.

"Which one of you Nasty Sons-A-B****** just freakin' farted?"

Andrew joined in as many of them were holding in their laughter. One of the young men stood up.

Trembling and shaking, he replied,

"Sir, it was me Sir!"

The Marine looked at him with disgust...

"YOU NASTY MOTHER"...

He caught himself before finishing the word that he wanted to say; then...

"BOY!... THAT'S 'YO FU***** MAMMIE!"

"Snickering" is heard throughout the room as everyone struggled to hold in their laughter! LOL LOL!

Next, the recruits lined up to get all of their hair cut off. Initial haircuts are a simple Buzz Cut. Nothing cute and fancy; just BUZZ BUZZ BUZZ as beautiful locks of hair fall to the floor.

Andrew walked the line as everyone waited their turn in the barber's chair. He was still chuckling inside about the recent "Fart Situation"!

As he laughed to himself, he had a flashback of going to the local barbershop in Visalia. He had his favorite barber, just like the other customers. Recruit Andrew Brown is advancing in the line to get his hair BUZZED OFF! At the same time, four-teen-year-old Andrew is approaching the barber's chair.

Deep in his flashback, young Andrew Brown spoke through the mouth of Recruit Brown, standing at the barber's chair. **Using his hands to pat his medium-sized afro!...**

> "Give me a Shape Up; Take a little off the top; And Line Up the back, but not the front, because I don't want people to see my big forehead!"

The military barber looked at the recruit in shock before replying,

> "SIT 'YO ASS IN THIS G-DAMN CHAIR AND SHUT UP!"

Andrew was embarrassed yet again (bwahaha-haha); however, nothing tops a dude wearing pink panties and another who farted so bad that the reply was

"THAT'S 'YO FU***** MAMMIE!"
HAHAHA

The men remained in the Receiving Platoon for three days of lecturing and receiving supplies.

ON THE FOURTH DAY

"Gentlemen, today is the day that you will be assigned to your battalions and your platoons!"

"When your name is called, answer 'Here,' then fall in line where those Marines are standing by the platoon numbers!"

Names are being called when

"Brown!"

"Here Sir!"

"Second Battalion, Platoon 2090!"

Andrew lined up with his platoon and is now ready for his Ultimate Test!

FIRST PHASE: THE SAND PIT

The recruits of Platoon 2090 stood in the room when a Drill Instructor (DI) approached. His uniform easily identified him as a Drill Instructor. The creases in his camouflage utilities, or 'Cammies,' were razor-sharp, and his boots gleamed like glass.

"PLATOON!"...

"A-yaaahhTen-TION!"

Young men snapped to attention as the DI spoke,

"When I give you the command to FALL OUT, you will FALL OUT and FALL IN on that sidewalk!"

"Give me four even rows facing me!"

The DI looked the men over.

"FALL OUT!"

They rushed out of the building and onto the sidewalk. Four neat rows of recruits lined up, awaiting further orders.

"Turn to the right,"

He barked. They turned, and the DI walked them to a three-story building. Located outside, to the right of the building, was a large pit filled with sand. The sand was smoothed over like a well-manicured lawn. (*It looked so neat and* pretty!...*Very Deceptive!*) They were led into the building's first floor and instructed to sit on the floor.

Andrew looked around the room. There were numerous bunk beds, foot lockers, and wall lockers. "This must be where we will be living," he thought to himself.

A Drill Instructor stepped out of the office, wearing dark green slacks, polished shoes, and a brown short-sleeved shirt adorned with his rank insignia on the sleeves and medals on his chest. His DI Hat sat prominently on his head, and a dark green belt was cinched around his waist.

Andrew gazed in awe, thinking,

"HE LOOKS LIKE HE'S STRAIGHT OFF
OF A MARINE CORPS POSTER!"

Two more Marines came out of the office wearing Cammies.

They stood in front of the men as the Marine in slacks spoke.

"My name is Senior Drill Instructor Staff Sergeant Martinson. To my left is Drill Instructor Sergeant Jones. To my right is Drill Instructor Sergeant Williams!"

"We are the ones who will turn you 'shit bird' civilians into Hard Charging Marines!"

"OOH-RAH?"

He asked the recruits.

"OOH- RAH!"

They replied in unison.

Drill Instructors Sgt Jones and Williams addressed the troops for ten minutes, telling them their biography, how long they've been in the Marine Corps, and how long they've been Drill Instructors. They left the building as Sr. DI SSgt Martinson stepped forward to lecture the platoon. He told the men his biography as well as some Marine Corps history.

He spoke in a calm tone as recruits looked in amazement. He continued his lecture.

"There are some new words and terms that you will learn in the upcoming days, Gentlemen!"

"You are not sitting on the floor,"

He said.

"You're sitting on The Deck!"

He continued with new words.

"Wall=Bulkhead. Door=Hatch. Bed =Rack. Bathroom=Head."

"That open space between the Head and my office is the Quarterdeck!"

The two Drill Instructors returned with a Marine recruit.

"This recruit is graduating from boot camp this Friday, and he's going to demonstrate the basic exercises that you need to know!"

The Drill Instructors called out each exercise as the recruit performed them.

"Push-ups. Mountain Climbers. Run In Place. Bends And Thrusts. Leg Lifts. Side Straddle Hops or Jumping Jacks!"

"Don't you ever say Jumping Jacks,"

They warned the young men.

"SIR, YES SIR,"

The recruits chanted.

The Sr.DI continued,

"Now, we're showing you these basic exercises for training purposes as well as disciplinary ones!"

He continued to speak in a soft tone.

"When you make a mistake, we'll use these exercises for Incentive Physical Training (IPT) as a learning tool and reminder!"

He spoke so nonchalantly that multiple recruits looked at one another and shrugged their shoulders.

"Alright Gentlemen,"

Said the Sr. DI.

"Playtime is over!"

He looked at the two Drill Instructors...

"Get 'Em Boys!"

The quiet and calm left the room when...

BANG BANG BANG BANG...

"GET ON LINE NOW!"...

"MOVE! MOVE! MOVE!"

The young men jumped to their feet in shock as both DI Sgt Jones and Williams carried an empty garbage can while banging the garbage can lid against it.

"MOVE YOUR LAZY ASSES!"

The men continued to furiously scamper to get in front of their racks when...

"TOO DAMN SLOW!"

"GET OUTSIDE NOOOOOOWWW!"

They lined up outside, wondering what was about to happen next. Then they hear,

"GET 'YO ASSES IN THAT DAMN PIT!"

They got in the pit.

AND NOW, LET THE FUN BEGIN!

Platoon 2090 found out the true meaning of Incentive Physical Training! The two Drill Instructors took turns barking out exercises.

"Run In Place... Side Straddle Hops... FASTER FASTER...Push-ups... Leg Lifts... Bends And Thrusts... I SAID FASTER!"

After twenty minutes of IPT, the recruits were breathing heavily from exhaustion.

The Drill Instructors halted them, allowing their breathing to steady after going back inside and taking a water break.

The recruits sat on the floor of the squad bay for another training lecture from Sr DI SSgt Martinson. He's thirty minutes into his lecture when...

"I HEARD SOMEBODY RUNNING THEIR DAMN MOUTH!"

"GET IN THE PIT NOOOWWW!"

"Run In Place" ...

"Bends And Thrusts"...

FASTER! FASTER!

Another twenty minutes of IPT. By now, they have sand in their uniforms, inside their boots, in their mouths, and in their hair.

This initiation went on ALL DAY! Drill Instructors Sgt Jones and Williams made every reason to take them to The Pit.

"MOVING TOO SLOW,"…

"GET IN THE PIT!"

"ONE OF YOU IDIOTS JUST TALKED"…

"GET IN THE PIT!"

The recruits weren't doing anything wrong. It's all just a part of boot camp. That's where mental toughness comes in. By the end of the day, the recruits went to The Pit seven times. They got yelled at for everything, and they were always "Moving Too Damn Slow"! In the evening, Sr DI Martinson sat the platoon down for another period of instruction.

"The average graduating platoon is thirty individuals,"

He said.

"Look around!"

They looked around at each other as the Sr. DI continued,

"There are forty- five of you!"

"That means that about a quarter of you will not make it!"

"Only the strong will survive!"

The two Sergeants returned with their trash cans.

BANG BANG BANG...

"GET ON LINE NOOOWWW!"

They lined up at attention.

"Get outta those stinkin' filthy uniforms, and get ready for your showers and Free Time!"

It's eight o'clock in the evening, and the men are exhausted.

Andrew got his hygiene kit and waited in the head with everyone else to take a shower. Suddenly...

"I HEARD SOMEBODY TALKING,"

Screamed the DI.

"DROP YOUR SHIT RIGHT NOW!"

The DI lowered his tone...

"Since you punks wanna talk so damn much...use your toothbrushes to scrub the head!"

"NOOOWW!"

Andrew thought,

"OH... MY...GOODNESS!"
"WHAT HAVE I DONE?"
"BUSINESS NOT PERSONAL...
BUSINESS NOT PERSONAL,"

Is what Andrew chanted to himself while scrubbing the head on "All Fours!"

After scrubbing the head with their toothbrushes for thirty minutes, the DI was finally satisfied and shouted,

"CLEAR THE HEAD!"

"CLEAR THE HEAD, AYE AYE SIR!"

They left the head still stinking and dirty from going to The Pit multiple times that day.

The recruits 'Hit The Rack' at nine o'clock covered in their dirt; but, no one cared, because it's time for 'Lights Out' Andrew was asleep before his head hit the pillow.

The next day was Day One of the Training Schedule. The young men were enjoying their sleep after the torture that they went through the previous day. Then...

"REVEILLE!... REVEILLE!... REVEILLE!"

"GET OUTTA THE RACK NOOOWWW!"

It's 4:30 am as recruits are startled out of their sleep. Now, one thing every man knows is that the first order of business upon waking up is to relieve the bladder.

Why DI Sgt Williams didn't heed this advice is a mystery to me.

Andrew stood at the urinal, relieving himself

while still half asleep. His head bobbed up and down like a 'newly potty-trained little boy' as he struggled to fully awaken.

For some ridiculous reason, Sgt Williams decided to play "Marine Corps Games" with the recruits....

"WHO'S TALKING?"...

"CLEAR THE HEAD RIGHT NOOOWWW!"

He walked up and down the aisle nudging. the recruits...

"I SAID CLEAR THE HEAD NOW!"

Andrew was still relieving himself. Once it flows, there is no stopping until the bladder is empty. Sgt Williams gave Andrew the same nudge...

"CLEAR THE FREAKIN' HEAD!"

The nudge threw the half-sleep recruit off balance. Andrew spun around from the nudge while still relieving himself.

He pee-ee-d all over Sgt Williams' pants leg with his head still bobbing up and down like a half-sleep three-year-old boy.

"WAKE UP, DAMNIT,"

He said to Andrew.

Andrew finally woke up to realize what just happened. The DI was so furious!

A few seconds later, he walked out the head to change his uniform while saying,

"As You Were... Take Your Showers And Hurry Up!"

The Drill Instructor must have realized his oversight, as he took no action against Private Brown. The recruits showered and attended to their daily hygiene needs, finally washing away the dirt from the previous day.

"THANKFULLY, I HAVE FIVE TOOTHBRUSHES,"

Andrew thought as he brushed his teeth.

The young men got dressed in their Cammies, and the DI walked them to the Parade Deck, where the remaining platoons in Second Battalion waited.

Platoons 2088, 2089, 2090, and 2091 were in Formation and waiting to be addressed by their Commanding Officer.

The CO spoke to the battalion...

"WELCOME TO PARADISE ISLAND GENTLEMEN!"...

"THAT'S RIGHT"...

"I SAID PARADISE!"

He spoke for fifteen minutes and finished by praising the young men for wanting to be Marines before turning them over to their Drill Instructors. Basic Training Has Officially Begun!

"First,"

Said DI Sgt Jones.

> "We're going to Medical, to find out
> how many Fat Bodies we have!"

Recruits lined up at Medical to get their physical measurements and body fat checked. Andrew's impressive measurements after his summer of intense bodybuilding training were:

- Height: 5ft 11in.
- Weight: 190 lbs.
- Neck: 19.5 in.
- Chest: 52 in.
- Biceps: 19.5 in.
- Waist: 29 in.
- Legs: 32 in.
- Bodyfat: 7%

> "I see that at least one of you came
> to Basic Training already in shape,"

Said Sgt Jones, as he pointed to Recruit Brown.

Andrew smiled within himself and gave himself an emotional Pat On The Back.

"JOB WELL DONE,"

He told himself.

It was painfully obvious that at least two young men had no business being in Marine Corps Basic Training. Their weight and measurements calculated their body fat at over 20%, which labeled them as too obese for Marine Corps training.

Sgt Jones questioned the failed recruits,

"What idiot recruiter sent you Fat Bodies here looking like that?"

They were immediately sent to Administration to be processed out of Basic Training and sent home.

"You need to lose a lot of weight,"

Said the doctor to the overweight recruits.

Sgt Jones approached Andrew.

"So, who are you?"

"Captain America or somebody?"

Andrew answered the DI...

"No Sir,"...

"But the Private trained with Mr. Universe John Brown during his summer vacation, Sir!"

Sgt Jones added,

"Well, you better not think you're special!"

Andrew replied,

"Sir, the Private is not special Sir!"

The following day was to check their fitness levels, which consisted of pull-ups, sit-ups, and a one- mile run. Andrew did 20 pull-ups, 65 sit-ups, and ran one mile in eight minutes. Aside from a few exceptions, the recruits of Platoon 2090 did very well.

"Not bad, Brown,"

Said Sgt Jones.

"Thank You Sir!"

Andrew reflected on the training that he did over the summer.

"One thing for sure is… I will not have any problems with the physicality of Basic Training!"

The first week of boot camp went by quickly. Their days consisted of Physical Training (PT) and Marine Corps classes.

Second Battalion performed PT together at 5:30 am, four days a week. They always began with the basic exercises to warm up; followed by a two to three-mile run.

As an alternative to the PT run, Second Battalion completed a barrage of physical training courses.

Andrew approached the Obstacle Course like a "Champ!" He ran through the tires on the ground like a seasoned football player. Next, he tackled the rungs of the Monkey Bars, reminiscent of grade school recess. The Uneven Parallel Bars posed no difficulty for Private Brown. He nimbly mounted the lower bar, balanced himself, and then effortlessly leaped to the upper bar. With a swift flip of his body, he dismounted with the grace of a Gold Medal Gymnast.

They went to the Rappel Tower the following week. Andrew climbed the ladder rung by rung until he reached the top of the platform.

Two instructors fastened the Safety Harness around his body. He's fifty feet above ground, and the only thing going through his mind is,

"DON'T LOOK DOWN!"

Thankfully, he didn't have a fear of heights. Andrew positioned himself properly as he began to lower himself. He stopped a quarter of the way down, then paused as instructed.

There's only one way to successfully complete the Rappel Tower. Andrew pushed his body away from the tower using his legs; Once...Twice... Three times.... followed by the chant, "Platoon 2090 On Rappel," as he began to rappel himself to the ground.

He held one portion of the Rappel Line in front of his body with his left hand, and the other portion with his right hand behind his back to be used as a brake when approaching the ground. Andrew completed the rappel while feeling like a member of a police SWAT Team.

After placing both feet safely on the ground, he gave a loud motivating

"OOH-RAH!"

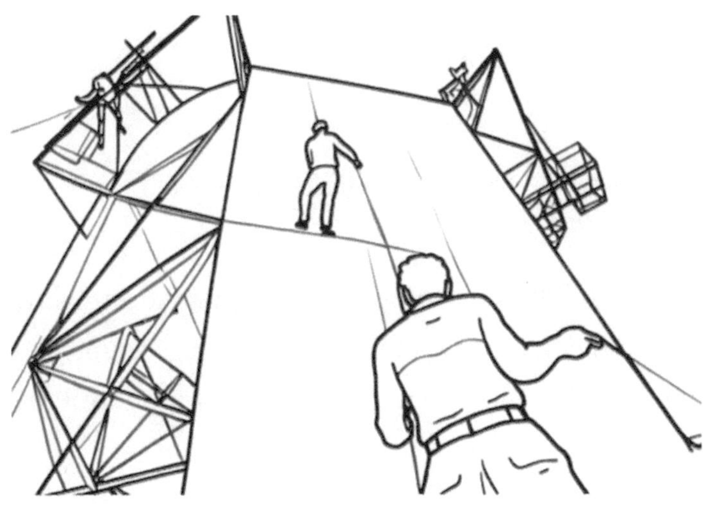

Their biggest PT challenge was the Slide For Life. Recruits climbed to the top of a platform about thirty feet in the air. A thick rope was attached at the top of the tower and angled down to the ground.

Private Brown laid his body on the top of the rope and began to "shimmy" down the rope, pulling his body with his hands.

The Drill Instructors gave him the command:

"Halt"

When he reached the halfway point down the rope. Then,

"Change hand positions!"

Next,

"Let your legs relax and rotate your body in the opposite direction."

Private Brown completed the maneuver while wrapping his legs around the rope again and continued "shimmying" down the rope until he reached the ground.

Another

"OOH-RAH"

From Andrew as he zipped through the Slide For Life with minimal effort.

Other recruits weren't so lucky; because, on the ground where the recruits were sliding from above, lay a huge puddle of water. Several members of Second Battalion couldn't complete the course. They didn't have the physical strength required and fell off the rope into the water. There were dozens of wet recruits after the Slide For Life.

Even with PT and military classes taking up a majority of the day, the Drill Instructors always found multiple reasons to yell and curse at the troops while sending them to The Pit for some IPT.

GET IN THE PIT! GET IN THE PIT!

It almost became a song. (*"I heard 'Get In The Pit' so much that I thought that was my new name!" LOL!*)

The physical, psychological, and emotional toll increased drastically as the recruits faced the grueling demands of their training regimen, which stretched an exhausting sixteen hours each day. They pushed through barriers, feeling muscles ache while their minds battled fatigue, clashing with their desires to prove themselves. Every moment was saturated with pressure, testing their resolve as they navigated through challenges designed to break them down and rebuild them as a formidable Marine.

The training was not just about endurance, it was a trial, forging mental resilience and forging bonds through shared hardship, as they stood together, united against the demands of an unfor-giving training schedule that seemed to stretch on endlessly. For Andrew and the rest of the platoon, exhaustion made sleep a welcomed gift.

The recruits 'Hit The Rack' at nine o'clock every evening. Hours of sleep passed by; when suddenly, whimpering and crying echoed throughout the squad bay…

"Mo-o- o-Ma,"

Said the shivering voice.

"I want my Mo-o-o-Ma!"

Everyone woke up, and the DI came out of his office.

"WHAT THE HELL IS GOING ON OUT HERE?"

The recruit continued to yell and scream for his "Mo-o- o-Ma!" Sr. DI Martinson grabbed the recruit and began walking with him toward the front hatch. He looked at the remainder of the platoon standing in front of their racks.

"HIT THE RACK!"

"HIT THE RACK! AYE AYE SIR!"

That recruit was never seen again.

A few days later, while everyone was getting dressed for breakfast, the Sr. DI walked into the squad bay and noticed that everyone in the platoon was dressed except one recruit.

"Get up here, Recruit,"

Yelled the Drill Instructor.
SSgt Martinson was wearing the same pristine-style uniform as the previous week.

He stared at the recruit.

"Why aren't you in uniform Private?"

Without saying a word, the recruit grabbed SSgt Martinson's uniform shirt. He tore his shirt open, ripping off the buttons and exposing his T-shirt.

"WHAT 'DA F*** IS YOUR PROBLEM?"

Yelled a stunned Drill Instructor.

The other two Drill Instructors came out of the office and began yelling at the recruit. The Sr. DI put on a fresh shirt and marched the platoon to chow while Sergeants Jones and Williams remained in the squad bay with the young man.

When they returned to the squad bay, the recruit was gone.

Several more recruits were dropped during First Phase for a variety of reasons.

As the platoon was getting dressed in the morning, the Sr DI walked up and down the aisle. He noticed a canteen on the deck under a rack.

"Why is there a canteen on the deck?"

He asked while picking up the canteen.

He noticed that there was liquid in the canteen.

"Whose canteen is this?"

Private Barnes stepped forward...

"It's this recruit's canteen, Sir!"

As the DI held the canteen, liquid ran down the sides. He immediately went into a rant...

"Did 'Yo Nasty Ass Piss In This Canteen?"

The remaining recruits looked at one another in confusion and disgust.

"YUCK!"

In an embarrassingly sheepish voice, Barnes answered,

"yes sir."

Individuals finished getting dressed for the day.

"FALL OUT!"

Barked SSgt Martinson.

As the recruits scurried outside, SSgt Martinson pointed to Private Barnes...

"Not You!"

"You Stay Here!"

Platoon 2090 joined the remainder of 2nd Battalion in the classroom after breakfast.

When they returned to the barracks, Private Barnes and all of his belongings were gone.

ANOTHER ONE BITES THE DUST!

MEANWHILE IN VISALIA

Andrew's mom paced around the house, wondering how her eldest son was doing in boot-camp. Despite his tendency to keep to himself, existing in his world of solitude, his absence at home resonated throughout the house, creating an emptiness that she didn't expect.

Each day, the reminder of his solitary nature loomed larger, causing Mom to miss Son more and more. Without him, the house felt not just vacant, but heavy with unspoken words and unrealized connections of 'What Could Have Been.' She truly missed her son.

Uncle Burney called his eldest sister, Andrew's

mom, who confided in him about the abusive treatment she had inflicted on her son.

"I shouldn't have treated him so horribly,"

She admitted to her brother.

She recounted how the abuse started when Andrew was just eight years old.

"I look back at all the terrible things I called him, and I am so ashamed of myself!"

She lamented. Uncle Burney tried to console his sister.

"Sis,"…

"It's not too late to tell Andrew that you're sorry for how you treated him!"

Sis added,

"I don't know how to apologize to him!"

"What do I say to him?"

Their entire conversation was about her treatment of Andrew during his childhood.

"Well, he has my address, and he promised that he would write me while in Basic Training,"

Says Uncle Burney.

"Well, you're his favorite uncle… I understand why he would write to you,"…

"But,"

She adds…

"I doubt that he's gonna write to me!" "When he left with the recruiter,"…

"He told me 'I Love You Mom' while giving me a hug and a kiss on the cheek!"

"He's never done anything like that!"

"I think that might be the last time that I've seen My Son,"

She said while sobbing.

The phone went silent as Uncle Burney began to feel sorry for his sister.

"I KNOW THAT MY SISTER WOULDN'T INTENTIONALLY HARM JUNIOR,"

He thought to himself.

He remembered his promise to attend Andrew's graduation from Basic Training.

He informed his sister.

After a long pause, Andrew's mom finally responded,

Andrew's mom went to church the following Sunday. There's no Andrew on the drums or the piano! No More Trumpet Solos! No More Flugelhorn! No More Euphonium!

She tried to enjoy the service, but the only thing going through her mind was...

"GEESH!"...
"THE MUSIC AIN'T THE SAME
WITHOUT ANDREW ON THE DRUMS!"

Mom missed her son at home and church.

As she stood there, deep in thought, she found herself slowly awakening to the depth of Andrew's character. She contemplated his quiet personality, his unwavering kindness, and his musical talents.

"I SURE HOPE THAT I SEE MY SON
AGAIN!"

Mom came home from church and went right to Andrew's room. She admired his artwork on his bedroom walls. Various drawings of Spiderman and The Incredible Hulk adorned the walls of his bedroom.

Mom looked at the posters of bodybuilders on his wall and reminisced about all the times that he would be training and eating to build muscle.

"WOW,"

She thought,

"ANDREW IS A TALENTED ARTIST."

She looked at the clothes in his closet and his

dresser. She smiled to herself as she began to see and understand his Humanity.

Although she wasn't snooping, she found the Love Letters that Dianna Marshall wrote to him.

Now y'all know how mothers are...

Of course she read my Love Letters!

(<u>You</u> <u>have</u> <u>my</u> permission to laug<u>h</u> <u>now!</u>)

HAHAHA!

MAIL TIME: RELAPSE?

During their Free Time, recruits prepared for the next day and wrote letters to family and friends. Mail Time is the highlight of each day. The DI called each recruit to collect his mail.

Today, Andrew received a letter from Uncle Burney— his first piece of mail since training began. Filled with excitement, he eagerly opened the letter.

"Hi Junior,"

The letter began.

(Only a select few family members are still allowed to call him Junior.)

Uncle Burney continued with the usual pleasantries...

"I'm Fine"...
"We're Fine"...
" Yadda Yadda Yadda!"

The letter continued,

"Your mom talks about you every day!"
"She said that out of all of her kids, you were the easiest one to raise!"

A tear fell as he recalled his last day at home, prompting him to wonder,

"HOW DO I FEEL ABOUT MY MOTHER?"

In the midst of emotional strain, he couldn't find an answer. Blinking rapidly to fend off the tears and memories, he continued to remember the abuse from his childhood as he drifted into a deep sleep.

Then, in a dream... Twelve-year-old Andrew walked the streets crying from the latest harsh words from his mother. He saw his father in the distance, and they walked towards each other. Andrew hugged his father... "Dad, It's You!" Andrew Sr replied, "Yes, It's Me Son!" Father placed his hands on the shoulders of his young son. "Now It's Time To WAKE UP!...

"WAKE UP!"

Private Brown slowly opened his eyes as he felt DI Sgt Jones shaking him by the shoulders, telling him to

"WAKE UP!"

Andrew woke up to find himself standing at the Quarterdeck by the Drill Instructor's office. The recruit on Fire Watch Duty spoke to the DI,

> "Sir, he just got out of the rack, and walked up here!"

> "He kept saying 'It's You' over and over!"

When Andrew was thirteen, he was frequently caught walking and talking in his sleep—a behavior that also occurred while he lived in Miami. The DI made him get back In the rack. As Andrew returned to sleep, he said to himself...

"I HOPE THAT DOESN'T HAPPEN
AGAIN!"

SORRY DUDE... THERE'S MORE!

The following morning, as recruits were getting dressed,

"BROWN...GET IN HERE!"

Rang throughout the squad bay. Andrew approached the Drill Instructors' office.

Before he could speak...

"Come in and close the door,"

Said SSgt Martinson. Then he asked,

"What's going on with this sleepwalking situation?"

Andrew wondered,

"HOW CAN I TELL THE TRUTH
WITHOUT DISCLOSING PRIVATE
FAMILY BUSINESS?"

He decided to tell a half-truth...

"Sir, when I was younger, I would walk in my sleep if I was in a strange place!"

"That's what happened to me last night Sir!"

SSgt Martinson replied,

"OK…as long as it's temporary!"

"But if it happens on a regular basis, you're gonna have to go to medical for further evaluation!"

Private Brown was dismissed, and he joined his platoon for the day's training.

Andrew did everything in his power to disregard the memories that were flashing in front of his face. He rubbed his eyes during military classes as his mother's slanderous words flashed in his face like flashbulbs from a paparazzi's camera.

The moderate Blink… Blink of his eyes increased to a rapid pace. He fought to focus on the instructor as his eyes…

BLINK! BLINK! BLINK! BLINK!
Like rapid fire.

His eyes itched from redness as tears began to flow. Andrew went to the bathroom and washed his face while crying uncontrollably.

"I don't know how to control this!"

"I can't have this happen right now!"

"I JUST CAN'T!"

He returned to the classroom, determined to get through the day's training schedule.

"I will not fail,"

He told himself.

Later that evening, the platoon finished their Free Time and 'Hit The Rack.'

Fortunately, Andrew didn't have any memorable dreams; thus, no sleepwalking or talking in his sleep this time. He carried Visine throughout the day just in case his eyes betrayed him by itching and turning crimson red.

"If I have to stuff these emotions deep in my gut to make it through boot camp, *That's Exactly What I'm Gonna Do!*"

SQUAD LEADER

During the training schedule, the Drill Instructors began teaching the recruits the Art of Marching and Close Order Drills. The recruits felt confused and unsteady as they attempted to perform the maneuvers.

"Left Face!"

"Right Face!"

Andrew, however, performed the moves with snap and precision.

"THIS IS VHS MARCHING BAND ALL DAY,"

He thought.

The DI continued,

"Forward March!"

"To The Rear…March!"

Private Brown marched with pride as he executed every command. He even correctly performed

"By The Left Flank and By The Right Flank!"

To call cadence for the troops, the DI speaks in a hoarse tone. Instead of saying "Left…Right…Left," the DI created a raspiness in his voice while calling his cadence…

"UuYef…Right… UuYef!!"

As the platoon marched in step, the DI guided them with chants that matched the platoon's footsteps.

"Lean Back…Set 'Em Down…Make A Rhythm… On The Ground!"

"UuYef…Right…UuYef!"

The better Platoon 2090 got at Close Order Drill, the prouder the DI became. Some of the

Drill Instructors even sang their cadence like a song...

"Yo Left Foot-a- 'Righty'-Doh-
Right- Left!"

The Drill Instructor's cadence made beautiful music as the recruits marched in step. Andrew took to Close Order Drill like a fish takes to water.

Unbeknownst to Andrew, his Drill Instructors were closely observing him and a few other recruits. His marching skills were the best in the platoon, and he often took the time to help his fellow platoon members with their movements.

Sr. DI SSgt Martinson sat the young men on the barracks floor.

"We're going to talk about
leadership for a little while,"

He informed the young men.

He began his lecture by telling the recruits the qualities of a good leader.

"Strong, Decisive, and Helps
Others!"

He covered an entire laundry list of leadership requirements while holding a piece of paper in his hands.

"When I call your name...line up next to me!"

He called the first name, second name, then...

"Brown!"

Andrew lined up with the other recruits while wondering,

"WHAT'S ABOUT TO HAPPEN NOW?"

A total of five recruits stood near SSgt Martinson. He walked up to the first recruit...

"You will be the Platoon Guide!"

"You're responsible for carrying, securing, and displaying the Platoon 2090 Flag!"

"Yes Sir,"

Replied the recruit.

He walked up to the remaining four recruits and pointed to each individual saying,

"1st Squad, 2nd Squad, 3rd
Squad!"

He pointed at Private Brown...

"4th Squad!"

"You four are the Squad Leaders for
the squad number that I just gave
you!"

SSgt Martinson faced the remaining recruits...

"Gentlemen, this is your Guide, and
these four are your Squad
Leaders!"

Andrew gave himself an emotional "Atta-Boy" and thought,

"DAMN...I'M GOOD!"

SSgt Martinson explained the duties of the Guide and the Squad Leaders to the platoon.

Andrew listened with great intent as he thought,

"THIS IS JUST LIKE BEING A SQUAD
LEADER AND SECTION LEADER FOR
THE VHS MARCHING BAND!"
"NOW I HAVE SOMETHING TO WRITE
HOME ABOUT!"

He wrote Uncle Burney that night to spread the good news. Uncle Burney, in turn, told his sister, Andrew's mom. As the young men advanced in the Training Schedule, events occurred that separated the platoon, sending the recruits in multiple directions.

For example, one group had to go to Medical, another to Administration, and on it went, as the DI had each Squad Leader march his squad to the places that they had to be.

Andrew had been waiting for this moment for over a week. He's been practicing calling his own cadence while taking mental notes of how each DI called their cadence.

Private Brown stood in front of his squad of eight Marine recruits. With his Baritone voice, he bellowed...

"Platoon...AyuuTen-Tion!"
"Ruu- iiight...Hace(Face)!"

I SPELL IT THE WAY I SAY IT!

YOU'RE JUST GONNA HAVE TO CATCH UP!!!

Andrew took in a breath, pulling a guttural tone from his diaphragm. With a raspy voice, he commanded his squad with a soulful cadence...

"AuuYorWard... UuYatch!"

"'Yo Left-Foot-A 'Righty'- 'Dohuu...Riuught-Left!"

Private Brown beamed with pride as he sang his cadence. His squad was amazed at his voice and at how "commanding" his cadence was.

During every break, his squad members asked him...

"How did you learn to call cadence like that?"

Andrew shrugged his shoulders while replying,

"I have no idea!"

"I listened to the Drill Instructors and just picked it up!"

He had a brief Deja Vu moment when his squad returned to the barracks. Later that evening, members of his squad were telling the entire platoon...

"Y'all need to hear Private Brown call cadence!"

"He sounds just like our Drill Instructors!"

It reminded him of...

"HEY SUPERSTAR!"
"WE SAW YOU ON UPLIFT!"
"CAN I HAVE YOUR AUTOGRAPH?"

Whenever they marched in a separate group, the word was always,

"Let Brown call the cadence!"

Nodding his head, Andrew thought to himself...

"I'M REALLY GOOD AT THIS!"
"I WISH THAT MOM COULD SEE ME NOW!"
"WHO'S WEAK NOW, MOM?"
"WHO'S TOO QUIET AND TOO SENSITIVE NOW?"

Even with all the good that he was doing in Basic Training, Andrew couldn't stop the memories from his childhood.

His mindset was always to "Prove Mom Wrong!"

POTTY MOUTH

The recruits had just finished lunch and were waiting outside the Mess Hall for their Drill Instructor. They've been on Parris Island for about five weeks. Now, one thing that Drill Instructors do very well is put their curse words together and spew them out in rapid fashion.

Platoon 2090 discovered that the cursing didn't stop with male Drill Instructors.

As the recruits waited for their DI outside the Mess Hall, a platoon of female recruits marched in their direction. Their DI was calling a nice cadence in her Soprano voice.

"Left… Right…Left!"

"Lean Back… Left… Right… Left!"

Someone from Platoon 2090 must have stared at the young ladies too hard, because...

"ARE YOU EYE F****** MY GIRLS PRIVATE?"

The DI was about 5' 5"... Lil Bitty "Thang"...

She walked up to the recruit, who was staring at her girls. She looked up at him while placing the brim of her DI hat on his chest. Then...she went into a cusrse tirade.

"IF YOU **"BLEEPITY BLEEP"** KEEP STARING AT MY GIRLS, I WILL PERSONALLY PUT MY FOOT UP YOUR ASS!" "WHO THE **"BLEEP"** DO YOU THINK YOU'RE LOOKING AT!"

The Private opened his mouth to answer when...

"SHUT 'YO **"BLEEPING"** MOUTH PRIVATE!"

"YOU EYE **'BLEEP'** ONE OF MY GIRLS AGAIN, AND I WILL PERSONALLY TAKE YOUR SCRAWNY ASS TO THE PIT!"

She looked back at her platoon...

"WHAT THE **'BLEEP'** ARE YOU CLOWNS LAUGHING AT?"

"THE ONLY REASON THEY'RE LOOKING AT YOUR UGLY ASSES IS BECAUSE THEY HAVEN'T SEEN A WOMAN IN OVER A MONTH...SO DON'T THINK YOU'RE CUTE!"

Private Brown held back his laughter...

"I don't want NOOOO part of her coming after me!" LOL!

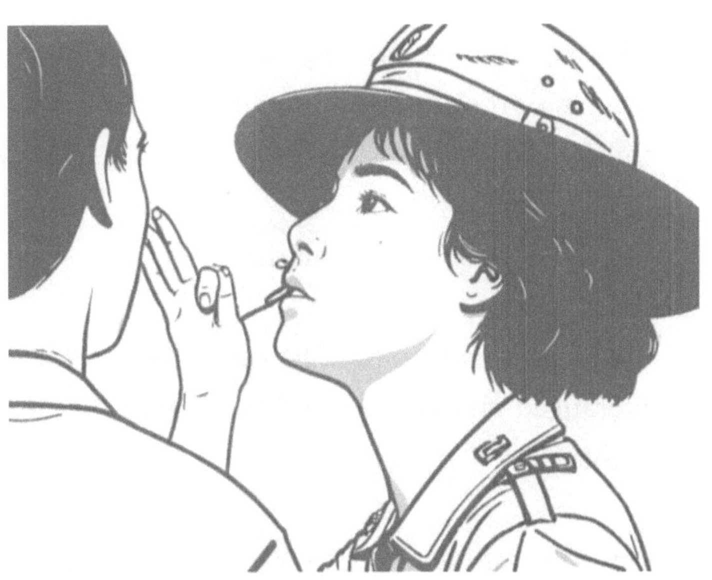

The men got to their next military class. The talk of the day was hearing that lady DI curse!

"I didn't know that they cursed like that!"

They continued the remainder of the day laughing at their platoon member.

"Duuuuude…. She cursed 'yo ass out real good!"

Andrew added,

"You got cursed out by a Little Girl"…

"Bwahahahaha!"

The squad bay erupted in laughter! Every recruit has their time in the "Eye Of The Storm!"

Today was his day!

Two days later, the "Eye Of The Storm" boomeranged and smacked Private Brown right in the "Moosh!"

Sgt Williams had the platoon in the barracks for a lecture. After he finished…

"We're going to take a few minutes to practice the proper way to salute an officer!"

He gave a salute, and held it...

"Do you see how my hands and fingers are straight?"...

"Sir, Yes Sir!"

"That's the proper way to salute Gentlemen!"

"When I stand in front of you... I want you to give me a proper salute!"

Sgt Williams approached the first Private...
He saluted...

"Good,"

Said the DI.

Second Private...

Third Private.

Now, Andrew has always been able to grow long fingernails. Some of his female friends told him that he had hands like a girl, and he liked how his nails looked when playing his Trumpet! (*It's a Trumpet "Thang"! "Ya'll wouldn't understand!"*)

While in boot camp, Andrew didn't take the time to trim his fingernails. Sgt Williams approached Private Brown... Hand Salute...

"WHAT...'DA... F***...IS...THIS!"

Sgt Williams held Andrew's right hand and brought it down for him to see.

"OH NOOOOO,"

Andrew thought to himself.

"YOUR G-DAMN HANDS LOOK BETTER THAN MY WIFE'S!"

"DO YOU WANT TO USE MY WIFE'S FINGERNAIL POLISH?"...

"SIR, NO SIR!"

"THEN CUT THOSE LONG ASS FINGERNAILS!"

Sgt Williams walked away, shaking his head. Oh

Yeah... You 'betta believe that Andrew cut his finger-nails immediately.' And that won't be the last time that Andrew let his fingernails grow too long! But that's another story for another time; when he had been in the Marine Corps for several years....

"Continue Please!"

"I'M REALLY ENJOYING THIS STORY!"

SECOND PHASE

Platoon 2090 successfully completed the First Phase of training and moved all their belongings to the second floor to begin the Second Phase of Basic Training.

First on the list...Rifle Range!

As the platoon made their way to the Rifle Range, Andrew found himself continuing to relive memories of his childhood. The flashbacks came at lightning speed, making it difficult for him to concentrate on a regular basis.

"Everything will be perfect if I can just Stay Outta My Head!"

Second Battalion was at the Rifle Range together as a unit.

Gun Safety was the Number One, Number Two, and Number Three topics.

"You Violate These Safety Rules, And Your Ass Is Gone!"

Andrew had minimal experience with guns, limited to a few visits with his 'Bestie' Samuel Johnson at Samuel's grandparents' house. Samuel, a deer hunter with extensive firearm knowledge even as a young teenager, had spent an extensive amount of time teaching Andrew about gun safety before ever letting him handle a firearm.

During each Gun Safety Class in Basic Training, Andrew thought,

"SAMUEL TAUGHT ME WELL,"

As the classes reinforced Samuel's lessons.

"THANKS, BRO,"

He muttered under his breath.

After Gun Safety Training, they proceeded to the Rifle Range. Now, the Range Master is in charge.

"THIS IS MY RANGE, AND YOU WILL OBEY ALL SAFETY RULES!"

He added,

"THAT GOES FOR DRILL INSTRUCTORS TOO!"

Andrew thought,

"I'M GLAD THAT HE TAKES FIREARM SAFETY SERIOUSLY!"

The range qualification consists of firing from 200 yards, 300 yards, and 500 yards.

They're reminded of the firing positions that are used to qualify with the M16 A1: Seated, Kneeling, Standing (Off Hand), and Prone. Next, he lectured the recruits on Slow Fire and Rapid Fire.

"Gentlemen, Slow Fire is when you fire one round...you wait for your score before you fire again; and on and on until you've fired the designated number of rounds for that portion of Rifle Qualification. Rapid Fire, Gentlemen, is

shooting the number of required rounds at one time; then you wait for your score!"

The first volley of recruits approached the Firing Line while Andrew waited for his turn. Butterflies were in his stomach.

"I sure hope that I don't mess up!"

The Range Master prepared the recruits to begin firing.

"READY ON THE LEFT... READY ON THE RIGHT...ALL READY ON THE FIRING LINE!"

"YOU MAY COMMENCE FIRING WHEN YOUR TARGET APPEARS!"

Seconds later... BANG, went the first shot. Andrew heard the BANG, and he was blinded by a bright light. Each flash contained images that he couldn't block from his mind.

BANG...Dianna Marshal!
BANG...Heartbreak!
BANG...Mom's verbal slander.
BANG..."YOU'RE USLESS!"
BANG..."STUPID BOY!"

Andrew's breathing became intense.

"If I can just block these images and these flashes of light!"

The first round of recruits finished firing, and now the second round approached the Firing Line.

Andrew took a Sitting Position to begin firing as the flashes of light continued at a much more rapid pace.

"I Can't See!"
"Steady Your Breathing Dawg!"
"Here I Go!"

The target rose, and all that Andrew could see was his face in the center. He rubbed his eyes, hoping the unsettling image would vanish. He fired a shot and awaited his score. Five Ring... BULL'S EYE!

"WHATEVER YOU DO,"

he warned himself...

"DO NOT DO ANYTHING CRAZY AROUND THESE WEAPONS AND AMMUNITION!"

Every target seemed to have his face in the Bull's Eye...

"As if I'm the target!"

During the day on the Rifle Range, Andrew functioned as required, but at night, he succumbed to a raging headache, dizzy spells, and tears flowing like a faucet that wouldn't shut off. He muffled his sobs with a pillow, hoping his platoon members wouldn't hear him.

Despite the intense training schedule, he felt compelled to 'Grin and Bear It.' He reminded himself.

"I'VE COME TOO FAR TO FAIL!"

Andrew was shaken out of his past a few days later when, as the recruits were enjoying their Free Time, a member of the platoon took off his jacket; then... (Clang Clang)... Five rounds of live ammunition fell out of his jacket pocket. All three Drill

Instructors swarmed around him, yelling and cursing at him. They called him every name that they could think of until they all decided to call him Private Gomer Pyle.

The recruit was escorted out of the squad bay by Military Police, and "Private Pyle" was never seen again.

After Andrew witnessed what just happened, he went to the head to wash his face. He looked at himself in the mirror, and with a stronger determination, he told himself,

"You Got This!"

"Just Stay Focused!"

"You're Doing Better Than You Expected!"

Two weeks later, Andrew qualified as a Sharp-shooter with the M16 A1.

"WHEW... YOU DID IT!"

Rifle Range-Check!

They went to the Pistol Range next. The only firearm qualification required was the M16 A1. The remaining firearms that they used were to get them familiar with firing various weapons. Andrew fired the .45 caliber handgun with ease. The final weapon was the M60 Machine Gun.

Private Brown loaded the weapon, and... BrrrrrrrrrrrrrrOw...a barrage of ammunition was fired at lightning speed. The butt of the weapon recoiled off his shoulder, leaving him with a series of purple bruises on his arms, shoulders, and chest.

He immediately thought about five-year-old Dirty Red in Miami with red and purple bruises on his body from playing and roughhousing with his friends in the neighborhood. (*"Y'all come look at this dirty red little boy!"*)

Next on the Training Schedule was the Live Grenade Throw. The recruits positioned themselves with their DI behind a concrete barrier. Outside the barrier is the sandy area where they will toss the grenades. Their Drill Instructors gave them one warning:

"If any of you decide to have slippery fingers after pulling the pin out of the grenade... I will toss your ass on top of the grenade and save myself by jumping over the barrier!"

"OMG,"

Thought Andrew.

He rubbed his hands on his Cammies relentlessly, until it was his turn to throw the grenade. The DI gave Andrew the grenade, and he pulled the pin.

"Fire In The Hole,"

Private Brown yelled as he tossed the grenade to perfection.

The remaining recruits tossed their grenades with perfection as well. It turned out that all the recruits rubbed their hands on their Cammies to dry them. *Smart Move Guys!*

The threat from the DI did the trick. Everybody's hands were "Bone Dry" before handling the grenade.

(<u>*Sometimes threats work!*</u>)

Second Battalion went to the Gas Chamber next. The DI gave the recruits a very deceiving orientation of the Gas Chamber procedure:

"When you get in the Gas Chamber, you will line up against the bulkhead. Then, when one of us walks up to you, lift your gas mask. Don't take the mask completely off; just hold it up enough to expose your eyes and the remainder of your face. Then you'll put the mask back on. After that, you will face the Exit, place your hand on the recruit in

front of you, take your gas mask completely off, and calmly walk out of the Gas Chamber. If any of you decide that you want to run out of the chamber, we will do it all over again...so WALK, don't run! "

"THAT'S IT?"

Thought Andrew.

"PIECE-A-CAKE,"

He muttered under his breath.

Then... The Monkey Wrench Was Thrown In!

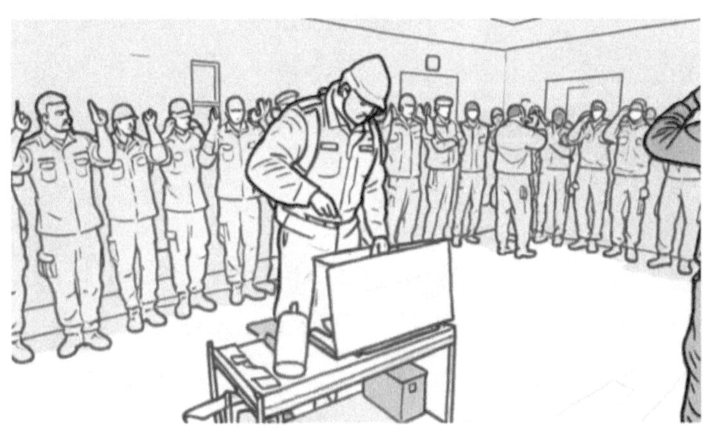

Recruits filed into the chamber and lined up as instructed. Everyone waited for the DI to approach them so that they could lift their masks up. Suddenly...

”Siddle Straddle Hops!”

Everyone looked at each other in confusion, thinking...

"HE DIDN'T MENTION THAT!"

"Side Straddle Hops Now! Run In Place! Bend At The Waist And Shake Your Head!"

"Now... Sing My Marine Corps Hymn!"

"From the halls of Monte"...

"Sing It Louder!"

"FROM THE HALLS OF MONTEZUU-UMA,"...

On and on they sang at the top of their lungs, which fogged up their gas masks. Andrew came to the conclusion...

"They're making sure that we're out of breath so that we can't hold our breath when leaving the chamber!" "SNEAKY!"

The recruits followed the commands and were

breathing heavily.

They lifted their gas masks, exposing their face while breathing hard from the exercises. Suddenly... COUGH... COUGH... COUGH from the recruits permeated the chamber. After completion, they began the process of walking out of the chamber.

"WALK. DON'T RUN,"

Andrew reminded himself.

Then, the DI ordered,

"OK...Take Off Those Masks, Hold Them In The Air, And Walk Out Of The Chamber!"

(*Sounds simple, don't it!*)

Andrew coughed profusely as snot, boogers, and phlegm flew out of his mouth and nose; but, he refused to run. Suddenly...

"Let Me Out,"

Yelled a member of the platoon in the back of the line. He began pushing those in front of him, causing a miniature stampede.

The recruits finally got out of the chamber when

"WE'RE GOING BACK FOR ANOTHER TURN!"

Andrew... Was... Pissed! They went back for Round Two, and they made sure that the Panicking Recruit was at the end of the line again. Thankfully, the recruits completed the chamber without someone "Losing It" this time!

When they got back to the squad bay, everyone was talking trash about the One Idiot who ruined it and made them go to the Gas Chamber twice.

Andrew wrote Uncle Burney that night to tell him that he had completed the Second Phase of Basic Training. He ended the letter with,

"In Another Four Weeks, I Will Be A United States Marine!"

Second Phase seemed to go by in the Blink Of An Eye! Andrew felt relieved to be able to get through the most dangerous part of the Training Schedule despite what he was experiencing mentally!

As the final week of Second Phase approached, recruits were enjoying their Free Time after another grueling training day. They were quietly writing letters and preparing for the next day of training; when suddenly, a loud scream of horror and pain pierced the air. Everyone looked up to see one of the recruits running towards the hatch screaming....

”NOOOOOOO!” “WHYYYYYY!”

He exited the building while yelling,

“I WANNA DIE!”

Several members of the platoon chased after him as he made his exit. He climbed the outside railing and attempted to jump off the second-floor balcony. Multiple recruits caught him in the 'Nick Of Time' and dragged him off the railing and back inside the squad bay. The recruit was crying profusely while holding several pieces of paper in his hand.

Within a few seconds, the entire room discovered the problem. His fiancée wrote him the one letter that no one wanted to receive. A Dear John Letter.

As Andrew observed what was transpiring, he walked to the head in order to not witness any more of the incident.

He's just three months past his own suicide attempt, and now he can't breathe. He leaned over the sink and splashed water on his face. He took a handful of water and poured it over his head. Water ran down his face, blending in with his tears.

The only thing that Andrew can see at the moment is one particular beautiful smile and Ebony legs 'Kissed By The Sun.' He's overcome with emotions as he says,

"LOVE SUCKS!"

With a

"MUAH,"

He kissed the back of his left hand as he remembered preparing for their First Kiss. Andrew smiled at the memory of his sixteen-year-old self, kissing the bathroom mirror during his self-created "Kissing Rehearsal!" He rubbed his feet together to play Footsies.

"I don't have my Footsies partner anymore,"

He said out loud in the mirror.

The DI and platoon members were preoccupied with the individual who just tried to jump off the second-floor balcony.

Andrew was slightly relieved because no one was witnessing what was going on with him.

"THIS IS THE LAST THING THAT I NEED AT THIS MOMENT,"

He told himself. Andrew slapped his face while speaking loudly...

"Come On Man...Snap Out Of It!"

He replied to himself,

"Why does Love have to hurt so much?"

"I was able to repress my feelings, and now this happens!"

In rebuttal, he replied to himself,

"Bro…Look how far you've come!"

"You're a Squad Leader, dude!"

"You have to finish the Task At Hand!"

Andrew shook the excess water off of his hands and returned to his footlocker. That 'Pep Talk' worked for the rest of the evening.

The next night, Andrew couldn't sleep. The recruit who tried to "Jump" was immediately taken to Medical. They admitted him for a 72-hour Psych Hold to ensure that he was no longer a danger to himself. Afterwards, he was processed out of Basic Training.

"I don't want that to happen to me!"

While the young men were asleep, Andrew slipped into the head and occupied a stall. He pulled tissue off the roll of toilet paper to dampen his tears. He also wiped away the tears from eight-year-old Andrew's face.

"I keep seeing the younger Me and it hurts!"
"Sometimes I don't know which Andrew is here!"

He finally forced himself to sleep.

The following night, he realized that he wasn't the only person with "extracurricular activities."

Andrew hadn't been able to sleep for the past three nights since his platoon member's suicide attempt.

It's one o'clock in the morning, the barracks is quiet, and everyone is asleep. Everyone except Andrew, who still hadn't reconciled his feelings about his mother and the 'Love' that he lost. He got out of the rack to go to the head so that no one could hear him. As he was walking, he heard a weird sound.

"Sounds like somebody just got slapped!"

He followed the sound as it got louder and louder.

"OH, THERE'S THE SOURCE!"

A member of his platoon was in his rack... Ummm... Entertaining Himself!

(Yeah, that's PG 13)

"Dude,"

Andrew said to the recruit...

"Go in the head and sit in an empty stall if you're gonna do that!"

After that, Andrew hopped back in the rack and managed to fall asleep.

Several days passed, and Andrew was still having trouble sleeping. When he managed to fall asleep, he had a variety of dreams that included his Dad dragging him into his coffin with him.

The next night, Andrew woke from his nightmare and went to an empty stall in the head. He carried a razor blade with him into the stall and made a bargain with himself...

"LOOK, JUST DO A TINY CUT...
NOBODY WILL NOTICE IT!"

He made a tiny half-inch incision just a few inches above his ankle. Tiny droplets of blood flowed from the fresh cut.

"MY SOCKS WILL COVER IT DURING
PT, AND NO ONE WILL EVER KNOW!"
"I'LL MAKE SURE THAT THIS IS THE
ONLY TIME!"

For the next week, he went into the head when everyone was asleep.

"JUST ONE MORE CUT… JUST ONE MORE TIME… I WILL STOP AFTER THIS ONE!"

He slept better after cutting himself.

"IT'S JUST A TINY CUT, AND IT DOESN'T BLEED THAT MUCH…SO I'M OK,"

He told himself.

"HOW DO I STOP SOMETHING THAT EASES MY EMOTIONAL PAIN?"
"PLUS, I CAN FALL ASLEEP AFTER I CUT MYSELF!"

Andrew continued cutting himself throughout the remainder of the Second Phase of training.

"JUST KEEP IT NEAR THE ANKLES,"

Is the deal that he made with himself.

"AND SWITCH THE CUTTING FROM YOUR LEFT LEG TO THE RIGHT ONE!"

(AND HE WAS DOING SO WELL… AT TIMES!)

ENTERTAINMENT: FIGHT! FIGHT! FIGHT!

THE TRAINING SCHEDULE INCLUDED SEVERAL FORMS of entertainment for the recruits. First, they visited the Base Theater to watch the 1957 Jack Webb classic, *The D.I.* The film motivated the recruits, evoking memories of their days in the Sand Pit during First Phase.

A few days later, they enjoyed another military classic: the 1979 Robert Duvall film *The Great Santini*. After the movie, SSgt Martinson addressed the platoon:

> "The Marine Corps Band and Silent Drill Team will be here in three days!"

Andrew, along with others in his platoon, were able to press and crease their camouflaged utilities to perfection but couldn't get a glossy spit-shine on their boots.

Others could spit-shine their boots very well; but, were unable to press and crease their Cammies to excellence. So, they bartered with one another. Andrew and another recruit made an agreement: Andrew would press and crease the recruit's uniform, and the recruit would spit-shine his boots.

Andrew promptly fulfilled his part of the agreement by immediately working on the recruit's uniforms.

Three days later, as the recruits were putting on their best uniform, Andrew approached his bartering partner.

Said Andrew, while giving the recruit his perfectly pressed and creased Cammies. In return, the recruit gave Andrew his boots.

They had the same buff shine that Andrew put on them three days ago. They were not spit-shined.

"Dude!"…

"You haven't touched these boots!"

The recruit didn't respond to Andrew. He just took his professionally pressed and creased Cammies, thanks to Andrew. The DI had them line up to inspect their uniforms and boots. All the recruits were 'Squared Away' except Andrew, whose boots weren't spit-shined.

The DI looked at Andrew with shock…

"Brown, you're a Squad Leader!"

"Why aren't your boots spit-shined?"

Without hesitation, Andrew told the DI how his bartering partner violated their agreement by not spit-shining his boots after Andrew pressed and creased his Cammies. The DI walked up to the other recruit...

"Is that correct?"

He asked.

"Sir, Yes Sir,"

Was the reply.

"Well then... You have Fire Watch Duty!"

The DI looked at Andrew.

"Fall In Line Brown!"

"You're going to the show!"

The Show Was Amaaaaazing! As he marveled at the Marine Corps Marching Band, Andrew recalled how the VHS Marching Band put on stellar performances every Friday night during football season.

The platoon returned from the show and continued with the remainder of their day.

Hours later, during Free Time, Andrew's bartering partner approached him.

> "You're A Snitch,"

He said to Andrew.

Andrew looked the recruit right in the eyes. With a grimace, Andrew replied,

> "You're the one who violated our agreement!"

> "I was not about to miss today's performance because of you!"

Andrew began cracking his knuckles while saying,

> "If you got a problem with me... We can handle this shit right now!"

> "Otherwise, get the f*** outta my face!"

(*Looks like Andrew* picked *up* cussin' *from* his *Drill* Instructors.) Several of the recruits were paying attention to see what was going to happen next.

The bartering recruit held his hands up while backing up,

> "OK, Whatever Man!"

He went back to his footlocker while Andrew continued with his Free Time. Andrew thought to himself,

> "I WISH THAT MOM COULD HAVE
> SEEN THAT!"

Thanks to Basic Training, Andrew was gaining the self-confidence that he lacked as a child.

He also became a little more aggressive...
In A Good Way!

OCTOBER 23, 1983: BREAKING NEWS!

Second Phase had been completed, and the recruits were doing their mandatory one week of Mess Duty in the Chow Hall before Third Phase began.

On October 23, they were two days into Mess Duty when...

"REVEILLE!" "REVEILLE!" "REVEILLE!"

"GET OUTTA THE RACK AND GET ON LINE!"

The recruits lined up, bewildered as to what was going on. While on Mess Duty, they got up at a particular time; but this is kinda early.

"Everybody come up here on the Quarter Deck and sit."

They followed orders as SSgt Williamson rolled a TV onto the Quarter Deck. He turned the TV on, and...

BREAKING NEWS! BREAKING NEWS!

Terrorists Have Bombed The Marine Barracks In Beirut, Lebanon!

Over 200 Marines lived in the barracks that was bombed! They watched the news coverage in shock, horror, and anger!

"I'm not a Marine yet; but those are still my Brothers under all that rubble!"

SSgt Martinson informed the young men,

"You're supposed to begin Third Phase next week; but, as of now, we are on Standby for possible deployment to the Middle East!"

He continued,

"I know that you all haven't graduated Basic Training!"

"No Worries!"

"Third Phase includes Field Training, and if called to report for duty, you'll be sent to Camp Pendleton, where you will get Field Training for a possible war against Lebanon!"

"Either way, Third Phase is a mere formality to officially becoming a Marine, and you will graduate early if military orders are issued!"

The recruits looked at one another with a sense of pride to defend the United States and to get retribution for those who took the lives of their Marine Corps Brothers.

"Shoooot"….

"I'm ready to go right now,"

Yelled one recruit. The remainder of the platoon shouted,

"Hell yeah!"

"OOH-RAH!"

They continued watching the news footage, and they were ready to fight this very minute! Even Andrew, "the quiet and sensitive one," was ready to fight! After two days on Standby, the Commanding Officer sent a memo stating that 'The Stand By Is Over',

> "And you can continue Basic Training!"

They didn't finish Mess Duty because of the Standby order. Now, Platoon 2090 is even more ready for Third Phase.

THIRD PHASE

T̲ʜᴇ ᴛʜɪʀᴅ ᴀɴᴅ ꜰɪɴᴀʟ ᴘʜᴀsᴇ ʙᴇɢᴀɴ ᴡɪᴛʜ ᴡʜᴀᴛ ᴛʜᴇ recruits were looking forward to the most: The beginning of getting their hair cut into a High and Tight. No More BUZZ BUZZ BUZZ!

Third Phase also provided a few benefits for the recruits. They moved to the third floor of the barracks, where a Universal Weight Machine was located.

Andrew used the machine religiously and gave training tips to the recruits who asked for his help.

Field Training is the number one priority of

Third Phase. First, Second Battalion went on a 25-mile Force March.

They were in full gear, with their M16 A1, and a fully loaded pack that weighed 50 pounds. It was a huge struggle...But they got through it.

They completed the march in the designated area to set up a base camp. Andrew and 'the crew' busily pitched their tents and established a Field Mess Hall.

Phobia: Squad Leader Private Brown was hyped during Field Maneuvers.

But Dude... Remember, You Have A Phobia!

Second Battalion was engaged in War Games as a training exercise. 'Capture the flag of another platoon, and you win!'

Andrew and his squad were determined to secure the flag belonging to Platoon 2088.

"Oh, I'm gonna get that flag,"

He declared aloud. Moving in 'Stealth Mode,' Andrew pushed through tall grass and bushes. He pulled out his binoculars and compass while spotting Platoon 2088's flag.

Advancing further through the brush, he quietly chanted his favorite cadence...

"Running through the jungle with my M16... I'm a mean motor-scooter, I'm a U.S. Marine!"

(*Yes...Motor-Scooter!*)

Andrew was fifty yards from Platoon 2088's flag and began to pick up his pace to a slight jog.

As he cleared the brush, he came to an abrupt halt. Just five feet in front of him was a large spider web, occupied by an enormous black and red spider.

Andrew screamed like a banshee, reminiscent of the shriek from the crook in *Home Alone* when Kevin McAllister placed that tarantula on his face.

(*"OK, you may laugh now!"*)

LOL

All that screaming exposed his platoon, alerting Platoon 2088. Thankfully, another recruit from his squad had taken a different path and captured 2088's flag. Platoon 2090 won Second Battalion War Games!

When they got back to Base Camp... Andrew got "Roasted" all night. Even he had to laugh at himself.

"Hey, y'all would've screamed too if you saw that big ass spider,"

He replied with laughter.

Now... Field Training is over, and the battalion was transported back to the Main Side in a cattle car. Only the recruits are in the cattle car. There's no DI supervision; so it's time for the recruits to have some fun. Suddenly...

"MOO,"

Says one recruit.

"Hey,"

He spoke out loud,

"We're in a cattle car, so we might as well be cattle!"...

"MOO!"

Then someone makes the "Brrr Brrr" sound of a bull.

The "Neigh" of a horse is next.

"OINK! OINK! SNORT!"

Says Andrew the pig.

Andrew laughed at himself while remembering the VHS Marching Band "Road Trips!" So, at that moment, there's a cattle car full of immature teenagers with no adult supervision.

HAHA!

They got to the barracks to finish the remainder of Third Phase.

Mail Time: Andrew's name is called to get his mail. It's another letter from Uncle Burney.

"I REALLY HOPE THIS IS GOOD
NEWS!"

Andrew opened the letter and began reading. The same Greetings applied in the beginning of the letter. UH OH...Here We Go Again!

"Junior, your mom has been admitted to the hospital."
"It appears that she had some type of nervous breakdown."
"The neighbors called 911 because she was walking outside yelling and screaming into the air!"

Andrew felt his chest begin to tighten as he continued to read.

"Psychiatrists and therapists thought that she was schizophrenic, but they eventually diagnosed her as Manic Depressive!"

Andrew's eyes filled with tears as he wondered,

"AM I SCHIZOPHRENIC?"
"AM I MANIC DEPRESSIVE?"
"IS THAT WHY THESE MEMORIES
CONTINUE TO FLASH IN MY MIND?"
"MOM MIGHT HAVE BEEN RIGHT
WHEN SHE CALLED ME THOSE
HORRIBLE NAMES!"

Andrew reached into his footlocker and retrieved the razor that he had been using to cut himself.

"NOPE...NOT THIS TIME,"

He told himself.

"I WILL NOT CUT MYSELF!"
"I NEED SOMEWHERE TO HIDE!"

Andrew walked into the head.

Recruits were still enjoying their Free Time, and Andrew was pleased that no one else was in the head.

He walked around the head, pounding his hands against his own head.

"I Am Not Mentally Ill,"

He said while looking in the mirror.

"I hope that Mom will be OK!"

"What if I have whatever she has?"

"NAAH!"

"I'm eighteen years old, and eighteen is too young to have a mental illness!"

He walked out of the head after washing his face, and then it was time to Hit The Rack!

One Hour... Two Hours... Three Hours passed, and Private Brown was still awake and weeping heavily.

"I CAN'T TURN THE TEARS OFF!"
"WILL SOMEONE OR SOMETHING,
PLEASE REACH INTO MY BRAIN AND
REMOVE THESE IMAGES!"
"AAHH, WHAT THE HELL...ONE TINY
CUT WON'T HURT!"

He walked back into the head while the recruits were asleep. Reaching for the handle to open the empty stall, he paused to contemplate the decision that he just made. The urge to cut himself was too strong.

"I have to cut myself…I have to cut myself,"

He said in a quivering voice.

He entered the stall. He has seven cuts on his left leg.

"I'LL SWITCH TO THE RIGHT!"
"REMEMBER, CUT VERY TINY ABOVE
THE ANKLE!"

Andrew cut two half-inch incisions into his lower leg.

Oddly, he was able to control his breathing after cutting himself.

"OH YEAH…THAT FEELS MUCH
BETTER!"

He patted away the blood drops as his labored breathing began to calm…

"NOW I CAN SLEEP PEACEFULLY!"

He fell asleep immediately afterward. That morning, Andrew woke up with the platoon and carried on as if everything was normal.

"I JUST GOTTA HANG ON FOR THREE
MORE WEEKS!"

GRADUATION: OOH-RAH!

RECRUITS TOOK A SERIES OF FINAL EXAMS IN VARIOUS military subjects. Andrew had always been a good student, and that hadn't changed. He "Aced" all his final exams. Andrew pressed and creased his uniforms to perfection for the Final Uniform Inspections. He glanced over to see his former Bartering Recruit struggling to press and crease his uniforms.

The entire platoon saw how he didn't keep his agreement with Private Brown and refused to help him.

"GOOD LUCK, CHUMP,"

Andrew thought to himself.

Second Battalion reported to the PT field for their Final Physical Fitness Test. The PFT consisted of:

- **Pullups: Minum Three. Maximum Twenty**
- **Sit-ups: Minimum Forty. Maximum Eighty. With A Two-Minute Time Limit.**
- **Three Mile Run: Minimum Eighteen Minutes. Maximum Twenty-Eight Minutes**

Andrew did 20 Pullups, 75 Situps, and ran three miles in 19 minutes and 30 seconds, giving him a score of 290 out of 300. Friday after Thanksgiving is Graduation Day! The recruits' Sea Bags were packed and lined up outside their barracks. Platoon 2090 marched to the Parade Deck for the last time. They fell in Formation with the rest of Second Battalion.

Andrew saw Uncle Burney's huge smile in the stands. Military Pomp and Circumstance proceeded the graduation ceremony. The Commanding Officer gave his final speech, and told the Drill Instructors,

"You may now dismiss your
platoons for the very last time!"

Senior Drill Instructor SSgt Martinson faced Platoon 2090.

"Gentlemen!"...

"Allow me to be the first one to call you United States Marines!"

"Platoon 2090!"...

"FALL OUT!"

The new Marines shouted...

"OOH- RAH!"

"Congratulations Andrew Brown Jr."

"You Are Now A United States Marine!"

"SEMPER FI"!

POST BOOTCAMP GRADUATION

Uncle Burney greeted the new Marine with,

"Congratulations, Marine!"

Uncle and Nephew hugged one another on the Parade Deck.

"So, how does it feel?"

Asked Uncle Burney.

"IT FEELS AWESOME!"

Shouted Marine Corps Private Andrew Brown Jr.

"Let's get your bags and get outta here,"

Said Uncle Burney.

They grabbed Andrew's two Sea Bags, threw them in the trunk of the car, and began the twelve-hour drive to Visalia, MS.

"Your mom is out of the hospital, and she will be so happy to see you,"

Spoke Uncle Burney.

Actually, Andrew was looking forward to seeing his mom.

"She's on a few antidepressants,"…

"But she sounded really good when I talked to her earlier this morning!"

Andrew forgot that his uncle was a smoker, and he smoked cigarette after cigarette during the drive. After Andrew's drunken incident, he hated the smell of cigarette smoke.

"OH WELL… I'LL JUST HAVE TO ENDURE IT!"

They stopped periodically for food, allowing Andrew the time to occasionally breathe some fresh air. They completed the drive in eleven hours.

Andrew's mom and brother Perry stood outside as Uncle and Nephew pulled into the driveway. Andrew got out of the car, and they greeted one another with a GREAT BIG HUG! Uncle Burney stayed at the house overnight and made his journey to Richmond the following morning.

"Thank You So Much Uncle Burney!"

Andrew's next Duty Station was the Basic Food Service Course at Camp Johnson, which is a secondary base as a part of Camp LeJeune in Jacksonville, North Carolina. He had eight days before he had to report to Camp Johnson, and he began to wonder,

"WHAT CAN I DO IN VISALIA NOW?"

Members of his graduating class, including his best Samuel Johnson, have gone off to college. His other "Bestie" Big O moved to Fresno, CA to live with his older sister.

By Andrew's third day home, his joy began to fade. Though he was now a Marine, he felt inadequate. As he scanned the house, reminders of past abuses resurfaced, and a frown formed as tears threatened to flow.

Suddenly, his closet seemed like a refuge. Andrew sat inside his bedroom closet, rocking back and forth.

"I CAN'T STAY HERE,"

He thought.

He checked to see if his old razor was still in the bathroom medicine cabinet. It was not!

"I should take this time to stop cutting myself anyway!"

Andrew's mom let him use her car, and he went to the only place that he could think of. Downtown Visalia. He drove the usual route, which meant that he would pass Dianna Marshall's home. He steered the car with his right hand on the steering wheel while crossing the fingers of his left hand...

"PLEASE DON'T BE OUTSIDE!"...
"PLEASE DON'T BE OUTSIDE!"

Well, that's one wish that would not be granted.

Andrew drove the Long Way, and there SHE was, standing on the porch. "Gollee," is all that he could mutter.

"That is the last thing that I wanted to happen!"

And sadly, she was outside when he drove past her house again on his way home.

"And Yes,"..." She's Still Fine As Hell!"

Andrew woke up the next morning...

"There's nothing for me here!"

If he wanted to fly to Jacksonville, NC, he would have to find a way to get to Jackson Municipal Airport. Plus, the closest flight went from Jackson, MS to Atlanta, GA, then caught another plane somewhere...

"OHNO!"... "I AIN'T GOING THROUGH ALL THAT!"

Andrew took a cab to the Greyhound Bus Station in Visalia, and began his journey to Jacksonville, North Carolina.

Three days later, the Greyhound bus pulled into the Jacksonville, NC Bus Terminal. To Andrew's surprise, a Camp LeJeune shuttle bus was there to pick up Marines heading to Camp LeJeune and the nearby bases. Private Brown boarded the bus, ready to embark on a new adventure.

"Hopefully I can keep my mind together!"

The bus pulled into the Main Gate of Camp Johnson, where the cooking school he'll be attending is located.

Private Brown began the Checking In process with the remaining Marines from the shuttle bus. They reported to the classroom...

"Welcome Marines!"

"Welcome To The "Basic Food Service Course!"

"This is a six-week course!"

"After you graduate from this school, you will then be given orders to your Duty Stations in "The Fleet!"

"This isn't Boot Camp Marines,"...

"We don't do all that yelling and cursing!"

"This... Is... A... School!"

Classes began, and Private Brown was "Off To The Races!"

The food service course was easy for Andrew. He had been cooking family meals at home since he was ten years old. He remembers the very first thing that he cooked. Ten-year-old Andrew wanted some scrambled eggs. He approached his fourteen-year-old sister...

"Geri, will you make me some scrambled eggs please?"

Geri replied,

"I can't right now...I'm busy!"

She added,

"Making scrambled eggs is easy; just go do it!"

Andrew got a pen and paper and wrote down the following recipe:

- Two Eggs
- 1 Tablespoon Of Butter
- A Dash Of Pepper
- Crack the eggs in a bowl and add the pepper. Heat a skillet with butter.

Pour the eggs into the skillet, and scramble them.

He started with scrambled eggs and progressed to making elaborate breakfast and dinner meals for his family. Fried chicken, collard greens, spaghetti with meat sauce, and a laundry list of recipes that were in his mother's cookbooks.

Beans, greens, tomatoes, (<u>ham</u>)... You Name It!

Everything was going fine mentally for Andrew as Chef School began. The childhood flashbacks began to subside, and he was thinking clearly for the first time in the last two months.

Then, he and several Marines from his class decided to explore parts of Jacksonville. The same shuttle bus that picked them up from the Greyhound Bus Station also offered rides to the Jacksonville Mall.

As Andrew 'Window Shopped,' the other Marines dispersed in different directions. The mall was packed, and Andrew took note of the bustling patrons. Mothers and fathers with their kids... Fathers with their kids... Mothers with their kids! **And more specifically...** Mothers with their sons passed by him as a young boy waved at him. With a smile, Andrew waved back.

The child is suddenly eight-year-old Andrew. Five minutes later, Andrew was struck with a flash of light like a lightning bolt! His eyes began to BLINK BLINK BLINK, and...

"I... CAN'T... STOP...THEM!"

He closed his eyes tightly in an effort to focus his vision.

Andrew decided to leave the mall early as he felt tightness building up in his chest. He was so blinded by the bright flash that he had to feel the walls to guide him as he walked out of the mall. As he walked through the mall parking lot, suddenly, everything went "BLANK!"...

"Hey, are you OK?"

Marines on the shuttle bus saw that...

"Something's wrong with that Marine!"

They approached him as he stood frozen in the middle of the parking lot. As the Marines tended to Andrew, he began yelling,

"I CAN'T SEE!"...

"I CAN'T BREATHE!"...

"I'M STUCK AND I CAN'T MOVE!"

The Marines caring for him suddenly began to float above the scene.

"I MUST BE HALLUCINATING!"

They're laughing at eight-year-old Andrew as pictures of his life bombard his brain.

"Can you make it back to the Base?"

Asked the bus driver, as the Marines helped him onto the shuttle bus.

"If you can, we can leave now, and I'll have you at Medical in ten minutes."

"I'd rather go to Medical on Base,"

Answered Andrew, as he struggled to breathe.

Ten minutes later, they arrived at Medical, and Andrew was rushed into the emergency room. After several hours of doctors and nurses "poking" and "prodding" him, the doctor approached him.

"You had a severe Panic Attack Private Brown!"

"You can get dressed now!"

Then...

"A psychiatrist will be here shortly to speak with you!"

"OH NO,"

Andrew whispered.
The psychiatrist walked Andrew to his office.

"Have a seat Private!"

As he took a seat, Andrew thought to himself,

"I'M JUST GLAD THAT THIS HAPPENED ON A SATURDAY, AND NOT DURING THE WEEK WHEN I HAVE CLASS!"

The doctor sat at his desk...

"So,"...

"We need to find the source of your Panic Attack!"

Andrew described seeing a Mother and Son walking in the mall...

"Then a few minutes later, my brain was hit with a "lightning strike!"

He filled the doctor in on the rest, and...

"This happened to me twice in high school!"

"Well,"

Said the doctor.

"We're gonna hold you overnight for further evaluation, and you'll meet with a therapist tomorrow!"

After a sedative helped him sleep, Andrew woke up the next morning. He met with the therapist, where he opened up a little bit more. He told her everything from being a child in Miami to his high school graduation. He conveniently left out the cutting on his body and the suicide attempt.

"IT'LL MAKE IT WORSE IF I TELL HER THAT!"

Well, said the therapist....

"I work with veterans who have a variety of mental conditions, and"...

"You just described the symptoms of PTSD!"

Private Brown looked at the therapist in shock...

"No Way,"

He said in confusion.

"I haven't fought in any wars to have PTSD!"

The therapist replied,

"That's true... But you suffered extreme emotional and mental trauma due to childhood abuse!"

"PTSD doesn't just apply to veterans who fought in wars!"

"Anything can trigger what you experienced!"

He was discharged from the hospital later, after the psychiatrist filled an anti-anxiety prescription for him. The psychiatrist and therapist gave him the same advice...

"When you get to your Duty Station in the Fleet, you should search for a psychiatrist and a therapist... and continue your medication!"

Andrew replied with,

"OK Doc,"

And returned to class on Monday.

Christmas and New Year's 1984 celebrations came and went. Andrew didn't participate in any activities on Base for fear that parents would bring their kids to the celebrations.

"I'LL JUST STAY BY MYSELF WHERE IT'S SAFE!"...
"I JUST WANT THIS TO BE OVER!"...

"I'M MENTALLY TIRED AND EXHAUSTED FROM THE WHOLE THING!"

His class graduated the first week of February

and received their new orders. The new Marines were all excited...

"Where Are You Going?"...

"What Do Your Orders Say?"

Andrew looked at his Marine Corps orders......

"Okinawa, Japan?"......

"WHAAAAAAAATTTTT!"

THE END
EPILOGUE: LESSONS LEARNED

It took Andrew a little time, but he finally finished telling his therapist how he made it through Marine Corps Boot Camp!

"Well,"…

"You did achieve your goal; but you relapsed and started cutting yourself again!"

"That's very disturbing!"

"You're lucky that you didn't get caught!"

Andrew let out the longest

"Siiiiiiiggggghhhhhh!"

"I know!"

"I thought that I had put that behind me; but, it resurfaced so naturally!"

"The compulsion to cut myself was too strong!"

"It's like I couldn't stop myself!"

The therapist continued,

"At the Jacksonville Mall, you had a Panic Attack so severe that it actually blinded you for about 30 seconds!"

Andrew jumped in...

"It's not as bad as it sounds!"

"It was the tremendous flash that lasted that long!"

"I thought it wasn't gonna go away,"...

"That's why the doctors said blinded!"

Andrew continued talking,

"The troubling part is that I still functioned at a high level!"

"Squad Leader in Basic Training,"...

"And graduating number five out of 44 students in Chef School!"

"That's why it was so hard for me to accept the first diagnosis!"

"Well,"…

"You're no different from anyone else!"

"Somehow you managed to pull yourself through"…

"You should appreciate that!"

"Yeah, you're right,"

Replied *Andrew.*

Then came a question that he didn't anticipate...

"Now that you're understanding your mother's actions, what about the possibility of dating and relationships?"

"Geesh Doc!"

"Why did you have to go there?"

Andrew had to be honest in his answer...

"I don't think that I'm compatible to date anyone!"

"I like who I am as a person, but, I always get stuck with the overwhelming desire to be by myself for long periods of time, and ain't no woman gonna go for a man who's not mentally capable of maintaining a relationship!"

"Plus,"

He continued,

"I still can't say that one particular name without being drawn back into my childhood and driven into an emotional frenzy, so, being single is the option that I've chosen!"

"I have Kobe now, and I don't desire to date at this point in my life."

"Honestly, it doesn't bother me,"

He added.

"Well,"

Said his therapist,

"You have time to work on that!"

"As for now, you're making really good progress!"

As the therapy session came to a close, Andrew's therapist asked...

"So,"...

"You went to Okinawa, Japan after that?"

"How was that Tour Of Duty?"

"OH Doc,"

Andrew replied,

"I'll tell you about that at another time!"

"Believe me when I say"...

"I've lived a very interesting life!"

LAVENDER JESSAMINE

From the Halls of the Island
Lavender Dreams continue
Visions of Camo
Entrap my new Fears
To the Shores of the Sea
Heart racing with worry
Drowning deep
In my Unspoken Tears

First to fight back the tears
Every time I see you
The Heart Loves who it Loves
No matter what I do
Stompin' in my boots

Walking out the pain
Memories last forever
I'm sick of hurting too

Always Faithful
With every breath I take
Dark becomes Light
It's never too late
No longer scared of the dark
No more sobbing for days
My Heart pulled through
No longer lost in the Haze

Magnolia to Jessamine
To Dogwood, Tiger's Claw
If the Rain starts falling
Accept no Fear of what I saw
With the raindrops falling off
'Tis be the perfect Night
Let go of what I saw
No more Thorns in the Side

Camouflaged Tears
Drown out the Cadence
Fighting Shadows
In the Silence
My Heart pulls through

Like Rhythm to the Cadence
I'm convinced
That I'm no longer Blue

Semper Fi! OOH RAH!
Anderson Banks, Jr.